WHALE SHARK

BY ROBIN TWIDDY

BookLife
PUBLISHING

©2019
BookLife Publishing
King's Lynn
Norfolk PE30 4LS

Printed in Malaysia.

A catalogue record for this book is available from the British Library.

ISBN: 978-1-78637-613-8

Written by:
Robin Twiddy

Edited by:
Kirsty Holmes

Designed by:
Danielle Rippengill

IMAGE CREDITS

All images are courtesy of Shutterstock.com, unless otherwise specified. With thanks to Getty Images, Thinkstock Photo and iStockphoto. Cover – Krzysztof Odziomek, vovanvan Kurmyshov, arka38. Boarder used throughout – arka38. Background Images – Ivan Kurmyshov, Andrey_Kuzmin, Song Heming, pirke, vovan. 2 – wildestanimal. 4 – Jacqueline Bodine. 5 – Lindsey Lu. 6 – Andrea Izzotti. 7 – Julian Gunther. 8 – Krzysztof Odziomek. 9 – Amanda Nicholls. 10 – Rich Carey. 11 – Rich Carey. 12 – Alexpunker. 13 – nicolasvoisin44. 14 – Ethan Daniels. 15 – Richard Whitcombe. 16 – ack_photo, Andrea Izzotti. 17 – Bill45. 18 – Leonardo Gonzalez. 19 – Christoffer Soederqvist. 20 – kaschibo, Napat, Lebendkulturen.de, BMJ, Allexxandar, 24fps. 21 – OutdoorWorks. 22 – Elsa Hoffmann. 23 – solarseven.

CONTENTS

WORDS THAT LOOK LIKE this CAN BE FOUND IN THE GLOSSARY ON PAGE 24.

THE WHALE SHARK

There are around 440 known species of shark. Some are small, and some are large. Sharks have **evolved** for millions of years to be the **apex predators** of the ocean.

BITING FACTS:
THE WHALE SHARK'S SCIENTIFIC NAME IS RHINCODON TYPUS.

There is only one species of whale shark. They are the biggest known living fish. The average size for a whale shark is 9.8 metres (m) long, but the biggest recorded was 12.6 m!

They are mostly found in the open waters of the **tropical** oceans.

TEETH

The whale shark has roughly 3,000 tiny teeth in its mouth! The whale shark's mouth is very big and wide. It can be up to 1.5 m across!

BITING FACTS:
SCIENTISTS DON'T KNOW WHY THE WHALE SHARK HAS ALL THESE TEETH, BECAUSE THEY DO NOT USE THEM WHEN FEEDING.

The whale shark's mouth is on the front of its head, which is ideal for how it feeds. As it swims along, it sucks in everything in its path and catches **plankton** and small fish.

NOSE

The whale shark's nose is hidden just above the top lip in the nasal groove. Inside its nose are barbels. These are like whiskers that are used to sense things in the water.

BITING FACTS:
SOME EXPERTS BELIEVE THAT THE WHALE SHARK USES ITS SENSE OF SMELL MORE THAN ITS EYESIGHT.

The barbels that hang from the whale shark's nostrils are thought to contain taste buds. It is believed that these help the whale shark to track food in murky water.

SKELETON

Shark skeletons are not made of bone like land animals' skeletons. Their skeletons are made of **cartilage**. It is lighter and more flexible than bone, allowing the shark to float more easily.

BITING FACTS:
WHALE SHARKS CAN SWALLOW UP TO 5,600 LITRES OF WATER PER HOUR WHEN FEEDING.

The whale shark has the largest cartilaginous (say: car-ti-LAJ-in-us) skeleton in the world.

BITING FACTS:
SHARKS HAVE SUPPORTING RODS MADE OUT OF CARTILAGE IN THEIR FINS.

Because cartilage breaks down much faster than bone, it is rare to find complete whale shark skeletons.

EYES

Even though they are the largest fish in the ocean, the whale shark actually has really small eyes. They are small and round, like a golf ball. This is tiny compared to the size of their body!

BITING FACTS:
THE WHALE SHARK HAS A SPIRACLE (SAY: SPI-RA-CALL) BEHIND ITS EYES. THIS IS A SPECIAL GILL FOR TAKING IN OXYGEN.

Unlike other sharks, the whale shark doesn't have eyelids. When it needs to protect its eyes, it can roll them back and suck them into its head.

FINS

All sharks have either four or five types of fin. The whale shark has five types of fin. These are:

Each fin has a different job. Some keep the shark upright in the water. Others help it to swim. The whale shark uses its pectoral fins to keep itself balanced in the water.

SKIN

Shark skin is covered in tiny, tooth-like scales, called dermal denticles. The dermal denticles all overlap each other. They are very strong and tough.

BITING FACTS:
SHARK SKIN IS ROUGH LIKE SANDPAPER!

The whale shark's skin is grey on its dorsal side (the top of the shark). It is white on its ventral side (the underside of the shark).

BITING FACTS:
THESE COLOURS CAMOUFLAGE THE WHALE SHARK AGAINST THE LIGHT SURFACE OR DARK DEPTHS OF THE OCEAN.

Its skin is marked by a pattern of dots and dashes. No two whale sharks have the exact same pattern.

TAIL

The tail fin is called the caudal fin. This is the fin that the shark uses to speed up and slow down. The whale shark's caudal fin is longer on the top than the bottom.

BITING FACTS:
THE WHALE SHARK MOVES AT A SPEED OF FIVE KILOMETRES AN HOUR.

The whale shark uses its large tail to swim through the water, by moving it from side to side. It swims slowly because it doesn't need to catch any speedy **prey**!

FOOD CHAIN

Food chains show us which animals eat each other. Most of the time, whale sharks are at the top of their food chain. This means they eat animals, but other animals tend not to eat them.

The whale shark feeds on plankton, **krill**, **copepods**, fish eggs and crab **larvae**. They also eat small fish and squid.

Very few things will try to eat a whale shark because of its size and thick, tough skin. However, great white sharks have been found with whale shark parts in their stomachs!

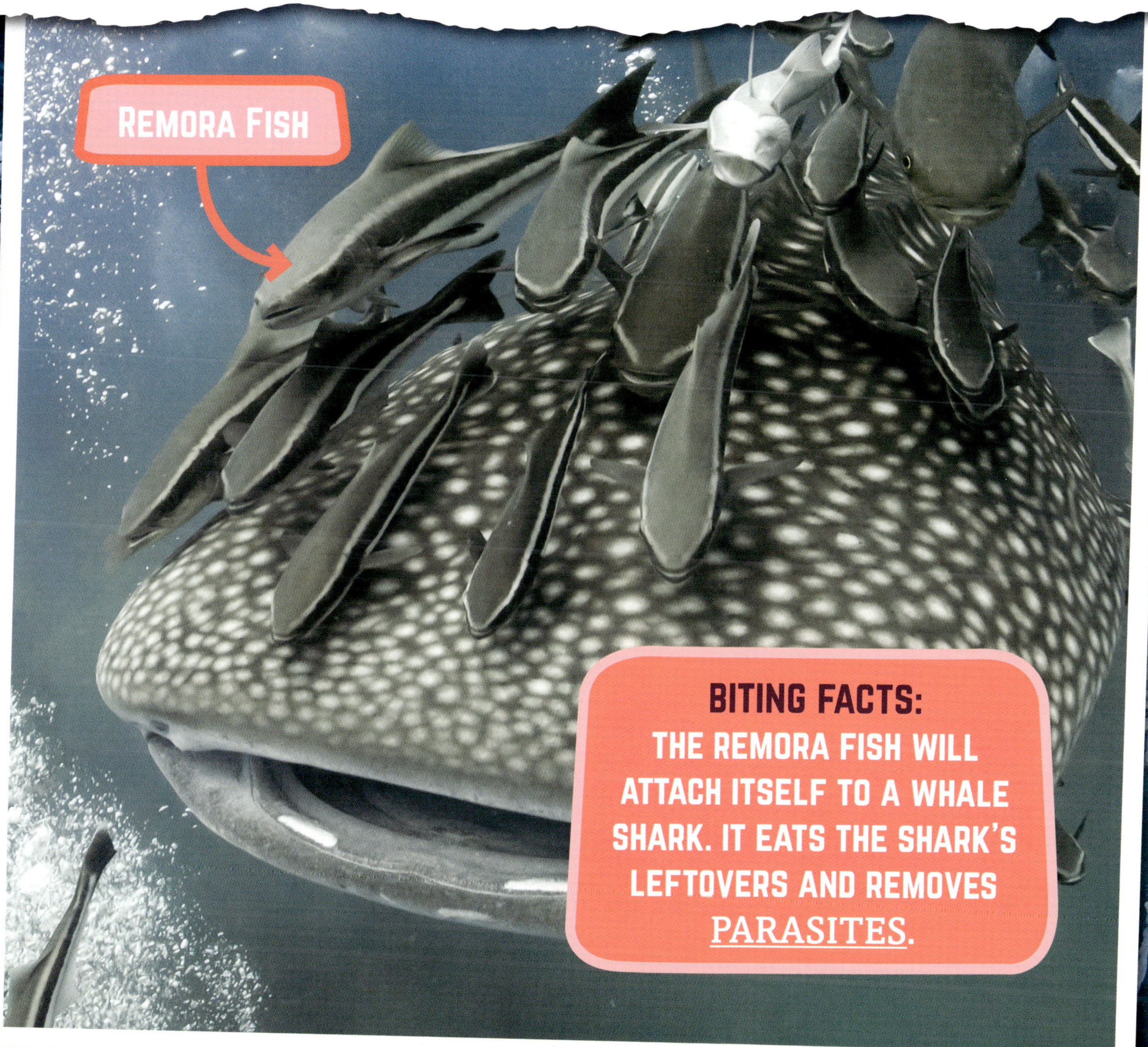

BITING FACTS:
THE REMORA FISH WILL ATTACH ITSELF TO A WHALE SHARK. IT EATS THE SHARK'S LEFTOVERS AND REMOVES PARASITES.

LIFE CYCLE

Most experts believe that the whale shark is ovoviviparous (say: oh-vo-vi-vi-par-us). This means that the babies grow inside an egg, but then hatch whilst still inside the mother.

BITING FACTS:
WHALE SHARKS LIVE TO AROUND 70 YEARS OLD.

Whale sharks can have up to 300 eggs at once. However, it is believed that the female whale shark will only give birth to around 12 baby sharks.

Some experts believe that the extra eggs are there for the newly hatched sharks, called pups, to feed on.

GLOSSARY

APEX PREDATORS animals that are at the top of the food chain and are not prey for another animal

CAMOUFLAGE traits that allow an animal to hide itself in a habitat

CARTILAGE a flexible tissue that acts like bone in cartilaginous fish such as sharks

COPEPODS a small group of crustaceans found in most saltwater and freshwater

EVOLVED developed over a long time to become adapted to a certain habitat

GILL the organ that some animals use to breathe underwater

KRILL small crustaceans found in saltwater

LARVAE a type of young sea creature or insect that must grow and change before it can reach its adult form

OXYGEN a natural gas that all living things need in order to survive

PARASITES a plant, animal or fungus that lives on or in another living thing

PLANKTON microscopic creatures that float in the sea

PREY animals that are hunted by other animals for food

TROPICAL hot and humid

INDEX